THE MABINOGI

MATTHEW FRANCIS

The Mabinogi

FABER & FABER

First published in 2017
by Faber & Faber Ltd
Bloomsbury House
74–77 Great Russell Street
London WC1B 3DA
This paperback edition first published in 2018

Typeset by Hamish Ironside
Printed in England by TJ International Ltd, Padstow, Cornwall

A CIP record for this book is available from the British Library

ISBN 978-0-571-33377-6

FSC
www.fsc.org
MIX
Paper from
responsible sources
FSC® C013056

4 6 8 10 9 7 5

Acknowledgements

ACKNOWLEDGEMENT is due to the following publications, in which parts of this book previously appeared: *Areté*, *The London Magazine*, *The Map and the Clock*. Thanks to Matthew Hollis for suggesting this idea in the first place, and for all his support, and to Creina Francis and my friends at Aberystwyth University for feedback. I am grateful to the Department of English and Creative Writing at Aberystwyth University for a semester of research leave to enable me to work on the project, and to the director, administrator and trustees of the Hawthornden Foundation for a Hawthornden Fellowship, which allowed me to spend a month at Hawthornden Castle completing the Second Branch. My source for the text was the Oxford World's Classics edition of *The Mabinogion*, translated by Sioned Davies.

Contents

Introduction

THE book generally known (ever since Lady Charlotte Guest's English translation of 1838–1845/9) as *The Mabinogion* begins with the description of a horseman hunting in a forest. He is Pwyll, prince of Dyfed in southwest Wales, and he has an encounter there that is to change his life and set off a succession of extraordinary events. The stag he is chasing is brought down by a pack of hounds from another world, uncanny creatures with shining white fur and red ears. Unaware that he is in the presence of the supernatural, Pwyll makes a terrible mistake, chasing them away and allowing his own dogs to feed on the carcass.

Already in reading this passage we modern readers have to make a considerable imaginative leap. We may, for a start, have little sympathy with blood sports; but hunting was the normal pastime for men of Pwyll's class and background at the time, the way they amused themselves when not indulging in their other favourite occupation of fighting, and there are to be many more hunting scenes in these tales. In our less chivalrous age, we are unlikely to realise at first the magnitude of the offence against good manners that Pwyll has committed in taking for himself and his dogs the quarry of another hunter, and particularly that of one who outranks him, for the wronged man, Arawn, is a king, not a prince.

Another difficulty we encounter is in understanding that Pwyll has crossed a still more significant line: that which separates our world from Arawn's kingdom of Annwfn, the Otherworld of Celtic myth. We are invited to suspend our disbelief in magic. If we refuse, none of what follows will make sense to us, for the consequences of Pwyll's transgression are entirely fantastical. They are also elaborate and far-reaching, extending in a dreamlike, elusive way over the complex plots of three more tales following this one, the group which describes itself, using the correct form of the Welsh word, as the four branches of the *Mabinogi* (the strictly inaccurate '*Mabinogion*' is now preferred for the whole group of eleven tales that share the same manuscript sources). This narrative logic, with its digressions and ellipses, is like nothing we are familiar with in modern fiction; it is the final obstacle we have to overcome if we are to take the stories to heart.

When I first read the *Mabinogi* shortly after coming to live in Wales in 1999, I appreciated the dazzling inventiveness of the magic cauldron that simmers dead warriors to life, the tragedy of the queen isolated and humiliated in a foreign country, the macabre wit of the would-be farmer trying to hang a thieving mouse using a gallows improvised from two forks. But I couldn't quite come to grips with the narrative as a whole; it was too alien and labyrinthine. Like any good protagonist of a folk tale, I have learned better since. These are tales that speak to us out of their own Otherworld, a world much older than the medieval manuscripts in which they were first written down, in Welsh, in the second half of the fourteenth century, the White Book of Rhydderch (*c.*1350) and the Red Book of Hergest (1382–*c.*1410). We may not know the identity of their authors or the precise circumstances of their oral composition, but if we respect their otherness, we will find, paradoxically, that they have much to tell us about ourselves.

Pwyll's unlikely punishment is to exchange identities with Arawn. For a year, he *is* Arawn, riding a strange horse, feasting in a strange hall, enjoying the wealth and luxury of a kingdom far richer than his own, while the man he has offended takes over the lesser realm. It's the logical consequence of the crime he has committed: take what belongs to someone else and you are staking a claim to be that person. Very well, Arawn says, if you want what is mine, you can have it, even down to my face and body. It sounds like a reward, not a punishment, and indeed Pwyll seems to have a good time during the year in which he assumes Arawn's identity. But can you ever really enjoy yourself when you are no longer sure you have a self to enjoy? In failing to respect the rights of another person and the laws that govern our social interactions, Pwyll has condemned himself to an existence in a shadowy domain where nothing is real, least of all the person who experiences it. This is both punishment and test: to get his own life back, he has to prove that he understands how people should behave in society; to earn respect he has to show respect to others.

The test has two parts. In the first, explicit part, he has to defeat Arawn's enemy, Hafgan, a man who, like Pwyll himself, has violated Arawn's rights, in this case by stealing his property and laying claim to the kingdom. Take over a man's identity and you also take over his problems and responsibilities – and Pwyll shows himself equal to this. The second part is more subtle. Along with all the other benefits of being Arawn, Pwyll is given permission to have sex with his wife, who, of course, believes him to be her husband. But this he refuses to do. In the daytime they talk happily together, but as soon as they are in bed, he turns his back. Touchingly, we see how hurt she is by his behaviour; indeed, the tale gives us, in negative form, a glimpse of a medieval marriage in which intimate conversation, as well as sex, was an important element. When Arawn returns, she reproaches him for ignoring her in bed, where they have always talked. In refusing the privilege that Arawn offers him, Pwyll shows that his understanding of human responsibilities goes deeper than verbal formulae, the letter of the law. He may have crossed one line, but he is determined not to cross any others.

This story, which, for all its richness of detail and variety of incident, is compressed to a mere five pages of Sioned Davies's fine recent translation, is a good example of the psychological and moral acuteness of the text as a whole. But it is much more than a parable, and Pwyll's experience is not only a punishment and a test, but an adventure, too. After all, crossing boundaries is something we can hardly avoid; living, as we do, surrounded by other people with their conflicting desires and demands, we are bound to stray into forbidden territory occasionally. And the protagonist who learns better has gained insights that would have been denied to someone who never went astray in the first place, as well as having had an exciting, if disorientating, time.

Pwyll's encounter opens a breach into the Otherworld, and, from now on, nothing is ever going to be normal. He falls in love with, and marries, a woman who has a mysterious power over time, and a mysterious affinity with horses. Their son, Pryderi, is kidnapped in infancy by a supernatural entity of which we see only the claw. Once restored to the family, Pryderi is to inherit his father's friendship with Arawn, receiving a gift of pigs from the kingdom of Annwfn which will eventually prove his undoing, as he is killed by their thief in a single combat at a forest ford that mirrors Pwyll's victory over Hafgan all those stories ago. In between, there are other boundary crossings, enchantments, forests, hunting scenes, love affairs, a whole war between Britain and Ireland, and a succession of fair-haired baby boys born in bizarre circumstances and growing up to have special powers. No one is quite sure what *Mabinogi* means, but it is probably related to the Welsh word *mab*, a son; though there are several strong and complex female characters in the book, particularly Rhiannon, Branwen and Aranrhod, this etymology suggests we may be expected to see its main theme as the coming of age of young men. Sometimes it seems as though we are reading the story of the same young man over and over, reflected in a series of distorted mirrors.

Pryderi is the nearest thing to a hero the *Mabinogi* has, but it is easy to lose sight of him. He dies near the beginning of the Fourth Branch, and is never mentioned in the Second Branch, though we learn in the Third Branch that he was present during Brân's war with the Irish. The tales are not a novel, and do not possess the cohesiveness that modern readers expect from a plot. Since Guest's translation, they have fascinated writers in Wales and beyond, inspiring, for example, Evangeline Walton's *Mabinogion* tetralogy, Saunders Lewis's play *Blodeuwedd*, Alan Garner's classic novel for young adults, *The Owl Service*, and, most recently, the *New Stories from the Mabinogion*, a series of eleven novellas commissioned from distinguished Welsh writers by Seren Books. On the principle that classics should be timeless, Seren have asked their writers to update the tales, requiring of them some inventive solutions to the problem of making these archaic elements – the social hierarchies and customs, the magic, the unfamiliar narrative conventions – work in a modern context. For example, Russell Celyn Jones and Gwyneth Lewis, in their respective treatments of the First Branch and the Fourth Branch, have reworked the plots as science fiction, feeling, no doubt, that a realist version would stretch the reader's credulity too far.

When Matthew Hollis, the poetry editor at Faber & Faber, suggested to me the possibility of a poetic version, I was at first doubtful, and a little daunted. I am neither a Welsh speaker nor Welsh-born. Unlike the Seren authors, I cannot claim the *Mabinogi* as part of my personal heritage – except in the sense that the greatest products of the human imagination are the heritage of us all. Rereading the four branches, though, I began to see how the very aspects that made a prose treatment difficult could prove a strength for poetry, which has never had much of a problem with magic. Poets spend their lives transforming things into other things. As for the differences in social and cultural background, far from requiring to be erased, they were part of the fascination. Much of my writing, in both poetry and prose, has been on historical subjects. Trying to understand the crafts of saddlery, heraldry and shoemaking that the exiled nobles turn to for a living, or explaining why a warlord needs someone to hold his feet at the banqueting table, has been, to a writer of my tastes, immensely enjoyable.

I have structured the book as four narratives interrupted by white space: the breaks between lines and stanzas, but also between larger units of text. Stanzas of five, four, three and two lines make up a sort of syllabic sonnet. Significant breaks in the narrative are marked by a large 'dropped' capital letter, which I hope will give something of the effect of an illuminated manuscript. The use of marginal notes has avoided trying to cram too much information into the lines of poetry, and should also help readers find their way around. As for the stories themselves, I have made a number of structural changes to draw attention to their under-lying thematic unity, and in the interests of the more straightforward narrative line that appeals to modern readers. Some episodes of the original have been omitted, and I have given Llwyd, the villain of the Third Branch, a different motive for his act of vengeance. The Fourth Branch is the most complex of all, and here my changes have been more radical. Taking my cue from the statement in the original that its protagonist, the magician Gwydion, is 'the best storyteller in the world', I have turned the branch into an after-dinner entertainment for a hall full of nobles and retainers. This gave me the opportunity to move the story of Pryderi and the pigs to the end, emphasising his role in the sequence, and to hint that Gwydion's repertoire includes all the other stories in the book.

As storyteller and magician, Gwydion knows more about the otherworldly kingdom of Annwfn, which I have translated as 'Unland', than anyone. Venture there even once, and its unreality starts to seep into our own world: a woman riding at a slow walk can outpace the fastest riders, an army can cross a river by marching over the body of their leader, an entire princedom can be whisked away under cover of fog, a man can make horses out of mushrooms and a ship out of seaweed. And the border of Unland is just over there, behind those trees.

The Tale of the Hunter and the Claw

HERE at the turn of the leaf a horseman is riding
through the space between one world and another,
warm in his company of noises:
hoofs, hornsqueals, hound- and man-cries.
Trees shed their dry brown.

He's chasing a disturbance of the forest,
a shiver passing from twig to twig,
the whispery commotion
of a deer running.

As he rides on alone and his men
diminish to distant shouts,
his hounds' song mingles

with the song of a strange pack
hunting towards him.

He follows the noise of strife. In the dogs' falsetto
joy and agony scrape the same fiddlestring.
He hears the forest wrestling itself,
the sigh of something heavy
kneeling to its death.

A beast the colour of bark lies on its flank
in the clearing. He catches its eye
as a parliament of hounds
meets at its belly.

Light shining through their red ears, they tug
and quarrel in the hot guts,
these white, unknown dogs,

Some of Pwyll's dogs while Vaulter, Singwell, Sidestep
cower at the edge.

[3]

He's up to the elbows in another man's quarry.
He's slit the stag's gizzard, unfastened his seams,
sliced, filleted, groped out the humbles
and laid them on the clean dirt
with bread sopped in blood.

Annwfn, the
Otherworld

He has shooed away the deerhounds of Unland
from the spread table of their own kill
so his own pack can guzzle
these filched chitterlings,

Arawn, King
of Annwfn

when a greater lord was after it.
Now his cheeks burn as he sees
a greyclad rider.

Arawn speaks

I know who you are, princeling.
I do not greet you.

Pwyll has committed
a breach of etiquette

Chieftain and chieftain meet in the still gaze of the stag,
who was a chieftain in his antlered country,
and this is shame, when your offal's spilt
among leaf rubbish, the blood
daubed on your outside.

Chief of a promontory of rock and woodland,
fields and sheep appertaining thereto,
suzerain of its townships,
hundreds and feoffments;

chief of unrock, unwood, of sheepclouds
and their pasture of vagueness,
suzerain of shades.

This is shame, chieftain, and this
is what you must do.

His punishment is to
exchange identities
with Arawn

You will wear my shape for a year now. Fasten the cloak
around your shoulders. Hang the horn round your neck.
Now swing up on to the dapple-grey,
who hardly fidgets, feeling
my weight on his back,

then look across to your own horse, where one sits
flushed with shame, blood drying on his arms.
You have seen his face before,
when you lived in it.

Being and being, beside themselves,
they ride out of the forest
into the grey-green,

then one is gone, and one rides
through a gleam of gates.

Pwyll arrives at
Arawn's palace

This clattering place must be home, these men hurrying
from the stables, his horse's joyful headshake,
their welcoming words, dungsmell, strawsmell,
cold air seasoned with woodsmoke
and roasting hogget,

how the strange boots love him, clinging to his calves,
in the in-between room where boots sleep,
the throng of muddied servants
wrenching him from them,

the heat in his face, the burnished light,
the hall rich in hubbub that
ebbs as he walks in,

Arawn's wife

and a smiling woman, dressed
in honey satin.

The cup is full again. He raises it to his lips
trying to read his reflection as he drinks,
a face adrift among candleflames,
unweaving his own voice from
the weft of laughter.

He talks despite himself, knowing all the names,
bandying old jokes he's never heard,
while his hand moves the knife, cuts
a piece of nothing,

which tastes of harpstrings and singing now,
the sweet stuff after the meat.
The song's about him,

firecrowned prince, warming his hand
on a stranger's hand.

Alone with his stony footsteps on the winding stair,
he hears his heart's footsteps running to catch up.
Walls blink and brighten as he follows
her will-o'-the-wisp candle
around each turning.

The room is many rooms, coming and going
at the whim of its flames. The red fire
utters yellow, and magics
a bed out of dark,

a cave hewn from curtain where they lie
in the candle's buttered light.
She is gold, silk, wax.

He feels her burn all night, through
the wall of his back.

He dreams he's hunting with the white hounds. The air makes way,
oaks bow him through, the dogs strike up their partsong,
he stops at the blood-draggled clearing
as the forest gallops on,
and it is no dream.

He stands on the tower studying the map,
the green and yellow squares of his fields
that won't hold still in the wind,
and it is no map.

And this is her hand, that voice is hers,
laughing and hurt. Every night
his back's turned on her,

and every day the forest
gallops around him.

You will wear my shape for a year. The golds of Unland,
harvest and chalice, harp and salver, forest,
and the queen of them all, shall be yours.
Days like sun on an eyelash
will squeeze into dark.

When there is only one, you will take my horse,
my men, and ride into the forest
to a place where the river
sprawls around white rocks.

Hafgan, another prince
of Annwfn
You will encounter an armed man there,
pesterer of villages,
worrier of sheep,

chief of unrock, unwood. This
is what you must do.

He rides, deep in his armour. He is joint, flange, rivet,
bassinet, gorget, the sword-jog at his hip.
The muffled wind rasps at his surface.
Two dozen men creak behind
in silverfish steel.

It's as he pictured it, the chestnut river
shaking itself loose, the juggle of flies,
the licked whiteness of the stones.
Now the sun picks out

a pinhead of light among the trees,
which splits into prancing sparks,
which become horsemen,

who draw up on the far side.
He calls for his lance.

In the slot of colour at the end of the long dark,
his enemy's a blob of gleam. He sees him
tugging his horse's head straight, and feels
the twisting of his own horse
wrench at his innards.

A mirror of air shimmering between them,
two riders charge into the shallows,
and the two halves of Unland
crumple together

to a point the size of a farthing
with the clang of a great bell
rung to smithereens.

A man lies against the rocks.
His head is crushed steel.

This is what you must do. This pesterer, worrier,
the false prince of Unland, can only be killed
with one blow. If you strike him again,
he will heal like a cut worm
curling into life.

He clatters across the stones to the smashed man,
prises off the helmet. Words gasp out,
the usual whispered request.
He raises his sword,

and sheathes it. A feeling sweeps by him
as of the air drawn backwards,
the trees unclenching,

as the man stares at his death
on the white-eyed rocks.

One chieftain returns to his townships, hundreds, feoffments,
to find the barns stifling with oily fleeces
or warmed from within by heaps of corn,
mills turning, lawsuits settled
by his other self,

and one returns to dungsmell, strawsmell, woodsmoke,
the hall with its hubbub and harpstrings,
and a cave hewn from curtain
in the buttered light,

where she sulks. Who has he been all year,
turning his back in the dark
where they've always talked?

A good friend, he says, someone
who's earned my respect.

Iᴛ's little more than a bump in the land, a footnote
in the catalogue of hills, crags and ridges,
felt as an ache in the thighs, the heart's
flip and gulp, by those heavy
with mutton and wine,

then a subtle sense of arrival, a breeze
scurrying up to attend to you,
the green swell of crown, the fields
gathering below.

They say if you sit on the summit
you'll see a sight more chilling
than the greys of rain,

or something more brilliant than
lightning's snazzy gold.

From up here, everything is cloud: the grass, forest, corn,
even the rocks, are nuances of weather.
The road's a white line through the billows.

Pwyll

He watches with his men as
a figure grows there:

a horse with a lick of sunlight on its back,
a horse with a knight in gilt armour,
a horse with a splash of silk
horsewoman riding,

not so much moving as sharpening.
Will she ever be real?
The boy he sends down

finds the road silent, her back
already dwindling.

Rhiannon

She is woman and horse. She rides slower than daydreams.
She is what you've forgotten, where the time went.
Singleminded as the sun, she rides
always one way, and the air's
warmed by her passing.

The man he sends after her, the second day,
tries slowing down; she rides slower still,
and the road grows between them.
He gallops again –

always she dawdles away from him,
till she's as small as a gnat,
and his horse gasping.

She slips into yesterday
without being now.

On the third day he rides himself, on his sleekest horse,
till it's yeasty with sweat. She is a brushstroke
on the stillness of the facing page,
illuminated in gold
on a green background,

and there is always a white space between them.
At last he calls out to her to stop.
There's a tearing sound, the sense
of a veil lifting,

and they are side by side, flank to flank.
He should have asked her sooner –
better for the horse.

They talk in time to the hoofs:
saddle-courtesies.

Later he will ask himself how she knew who he was,
and why she chose him out of all the princes
who hunt under these lumbering clouds.
Now he is watching her smile
as it comes and goes,

a slip of candlelight seen under a door,
listening to the cluck of laughter
that nestles deep in her throat,
hearing himself talk

in the silences she leaves for him.
Later they will feast and dance
and climb the long stairs.

Later he'll wonder. Today
there's wonder enough.

*The newborn son of
Pwyll and Rhiannon*

SLEEP, wrinkled princeling, after the months clenched in the
  dark,
in your unfamiliar palaceful of air.
Now there's a candle's eye to watch you,
the two eyes of a woman
to shine on your sleep,

five more women to knit their breath around you,
a sleeping chamberful of mothers.
The hound bitch in the corner
snuggles with her pups,

as the palace whimpers in its sleep,
Nursemaids   and six women, through the night,
sleep and wake in turn.

Sleep as your mother's sleeping,
a curtain away.

All six women have the same dream. They have lost something,
a ring, a stone. They're overturning cushions,
rustling through the rushes on the floor,
as an intruder draws near.
It's in the room now,

a white presence they recognise as daybreak.
It's too late. They look at each other
and see there are six of them.
One should be awake.

They fall out of the dream with a gasp
to find the whiteness still there.
They already know

*The young prince
has been magically
abducted*

what they'll find in the cradle:
his crumpled linen.

Such a small difference between here and gone. They can't
    breathe.
Perhaps they can think him back, or unthink him,
so there's nothing, nobody, to lose.
In every world but this one
the light grows richer,

the greens and reds appear in the tapestries,
and the day is sweet with his crying
or wholesome in its silence.
In this world they wait

*The women are afraid
of punishment*

for the stirring behind the curtain
and what will happen after:
dungeons, whips, burning.

There's no crack in the glass walls
of here, themselves, now.

One mother sleeps in the newborn light – it's not morning
in the darkness she has woven for herself,
though the threads are beginning to fray.
The whispers she hears outside
aren't the birds singing.

One is stretched in the corner, fused to her pups,
fur garment with too many tassels,
map of an unknown island,
all frilly coastline.

And six fetch a knife from the kitchen
and prise three pups from the teats –
plump slippers of warmth –

puddle their blood on the floor,
heap up the small bones.

She's slept too long. A draught is fingering her nightgown.
Her son is crying somewhere, or he's just stopped.
The fresh silence beyond the curtain
still bears the traces of it,
scratches in her mind.

Where is the boy who filled the room with his breath,
my women? What are you staring at?
What is that red on the floor,
that puzzle of bones?

The women blame
Rhiannon

We've struggled with a nightmare, lady,
a woman white as the moon,
who wrenched him from us.

The blood and bones are your son;
the nightmare was you.

Under the overhang of old smoke, a new fire's lit,
the same colour as the sun-streaks in the hall.
He tastes the morning ale, half his mind
on hunting, half on his child.
A moment from now,

a boy will come, bowing, bumping the table,
fighting his lungs for the words, one flick
of hair askew on his brow.
A moment later,

he will plunge through the void of himself,
run through his faraway home
to a wailing room,

but this moment is blue smoke,
new fire, morning ale.

Long-legged, she squats in the dust by the mounting-block,
staring for hours at something behind the air,
the way animals do. Speak to her,
stranger, and she'll shake her head
to swish off the flies.

She'll carry you on her back, if you'll let her,
the last mile to her husband's castle.
It was their word against hers,
six frightened women,

and she's no longer sure what she did.
It's meant as a punishment,
this life of burdens.

To her it seems a return
to a strong-boned self.

THIS is horse country. They loiter in the shrunken fields
    beneath low hills, as naked as the river,
off-duty, three or four to a herd.
Grazing, they seem half-asleep,
sleeping, like statues.

And the lord here measures his wealth in horses:
the hundreds of common brutes he owns,
the dynasties of pure-bloods,
and his one arch-horse,

a mare with a cataract of mane
and a hide of watered silk,
the last of her line –

each May Eve she gives birth, then
the foal vanishes.

The earth is brewing its new beer, a froth of daisies,
and the rabbits in the fields are drunk with it.
There's a green smell in the lukewarm breeze.
It will be May tomorrow:
tonight she gives birth.

This time he'll watch through the night – not in the dark,
but in the hall with torches burning
and a platoon of armed men
standing all round her.

They make a nest of hay by the fire
and she subsides into it,
beached on her ribcage,

her eyes reflecting the flames,
her nostrils staring.

Night gets its own way in the end. The torches go out,
the fire burns down to its internal organs,
and the hall is charcoal and darkness.
His mind shrinks as the heat dies,
a ticking ember.

A horse is crying nearby. He is afloat
on the amber puddle of its tears.
He hears the sound of struggling,
and tries to wake up.

Where there was horse a white flower looms,
and in the flower two hoofs
and a narrow face,

and then the lying-down dance
of four stalky legs.

The legs are scrabbling at random, in search of the floor,
rebounding off hardness, losing it again,
so the foal tries to stand without them,
a snake of head and body.
The legs won't have it.

They wedge themselves underneath, and the foal's launched
on to the heaving sea of upright,
fighting to lock his loose parts
into solid horse,

like the mother beside him, who licks
the wetness off him, shaping
his limbs with her tongue,

till he can stand on all-fours,
holding the world down.

The timbers sway and crack. A gale's trying to get in.
Its nails scrape the roof, its muzzle's at the door,
it has the shapeless voice of a crow.
The prince stands with his sword drawn
to hack at the wind.

He's heard it all his life. Now it's a stranger,
shushing itself outside the window,
balked at first by its smallness,
creaking and fumbling,

feeling for the gap with clawed fingers
that tiptoe inside, glossy
in the reddish glare,

on the end of a long beam
of scaly forearm.

A monstrous claw tries
to seize the foal

A horny, dimpled claw, its palm the size of a shield,
it pauses, lifting the arch of one finger,
as if seeing the man watching it,
then spiders across the floor
to where the foal stands,

beside the bulky shadow of its mother.
Pivoting on the thumb, it rears up
and twines itself in the mane.
Hoofs kick at nothing.

Both horses scream at this second birth.
He sees the arm pulling back
and strikes with the sword.

It's severed at the elbow,
clean as a new cheese.

The arm falls bloodless to the floor, the foal in its grip,
and the prince runs into the bellowing dark,
where there's no creature to struggle with,
unless it's all around him.
Behind him, the door's

an open wound, leaking the red of firelight.
Going back to see to it, he finds
a long cocoon of gold silk
laid on the threshold,

the face of a baby staring out.
This is the boy he will raise:
child of a maimed beast,

foster-brother to a horse,
night's yellow hatchling.

*Gwri Wallt Euryn
(Gwri of the Golden
Hair), the child
dropped by the claw*

He thinks with his legs, will run away in mid-sentence,
as if the next field were an idea. He eats
head down, studying the book of food.
He is growing on purpose.
He loves the moist gloom

of the stables, intimate as a nostril,
the great horses his uncles and aunts,
the stripling horse his brother.
They talk nose to nose.

He is the son of the house, carries
his still, white face through its hall.
Where does it come from?

It is the face of a prince,
but not of these parts.

Teyrnon's wife   Sometimes she wakes with a dream between her and the light,
always a miniature human form, floating
in the watery land of her eyes
among bright stems of lashes.
A blink dissolves it.

The boy was like that, the floater of a dream,
as she was to him. When she held him
she saw him blink her away,
felt the world swimming.

Gwri is the missing   So when her husband comes to tell her
child   of a lost child in the west,
a broken mother,

the morning hardens to glass,
and her eyes are clear.

A long-maned woman in the dust by the mounting block
tells them to leave their horses. She'll be their horse.
They've been riding all day. The sky is
sweetened with red, like the flesh
of summer apples,

and the grey castle on its mound looms and fades
so that almost there seems a long way.
No woman will carry them,
they're resolved on that.

She stands with an unfolding movement
that reminds them of something,
but won't meet their eyes,

The boy is restored to   the lord, his colt of a son.
his parents   And then she sees him.

Pwyll

HERE at the turn of the leaf the chieftain is hunting,
forgetting townships and hundreds, fields and sheep,
the wife and son back in his castle,
chasing a whisper of deer
through his brown woodlands.

Rhiannon

His wife's in her room stretching a tawny thread
through the embroidered neck of a horse.
The day grows long as she pulls,
short when she pushes.

Pryderi (Gwri)

And the boy she has renamed Worry
for what he has been to her
rides his father's land,

murmuring into the ear
of his brother horse.

THE SECOND BRANCH

The Tale of the Queen and the Cauldron

HE is the capital at the start of the sentence,
a tree, a crow's nest, a furlong of a man.
You cannot think of him all at once.
Picture his scrubland of beard,
his battlement teeth.

Or think of the vertigo of standing there
gazing from the parapet of self
he can never climb down from,
the wind in his ears

that his friends must shout to compete with,
a life lived in the weather –
no house will hold him.

He is closer to the birds
than his family.

He feels a kinship with high places. Here on the cliffs
he can watch the sea think its blue and grey thoughts.
Sometimes crazed causeways appear in it
or creeping patches of dark
trouble the surface.

Today there's a grainy cloud in the distance
that might be a swirl of mosquitoes
picking the sun to pieces
with their bits of wings,

but whiter, more bosomy than that:
a flotilla of seagulls,
salt-water swans?

More complicated than that –
it's something human.

The wind fluttering through a volume of blank pages –
thirteen ships approaching from the smudgy west,
where there is known to be an island
dangerously like this one,
but darker, vaguer.

Ireland

Their jauntiness disturbs him, those puffs of cloth
and the banners squiggling above them,
unreadable signatures
in red, green and gold.

They have come as close as they can now,
and are busy with a task
he can't see or hear,

till the smooth blue breaks into
a rash of black boats.

A diplomatic mission

These are the manners of kings: to raise a shield point-up
on the mainmast as a sign you come in peace;
to stay on the ship till asked ashore;
to send out messengers to
the sandy threshold,

where they must shout politely up the cliff face
to the one who seems carved out of it
to this effect: All the world
acknowledges the . . .

The Irish king hopes to marry Branwen, sister of Brân

of Her Grace His Grace's sister, who . . .
no woman . . . the whiteness of . . .
her gentle . . . to which . . .

of our two peoples . . . strengthened . . .
these unworthy gifts . . .

They come ashore all day, making a noise like language,
laughing as if they want everyone to hear,
rucking up the beach with their footprints,
humping nailed-up crates, trundling
cartloads of clatter.

Outside the town a distant prospect of tent,
the late sun embroidering its skirts,
the lightning of cooking-fires,
nimbus of woodsmoke.

Matholwch, King
of Ireland

The strange king sits beside his host's knees
and looks up into the tent's
inverted abyss,

reaching out for the cold hand
of his one-hour's bride.

What is a man without horses? He's brought his with him.
At every stable they are towelled and burnished,
honoured with the heaped hay of the trough
by their grooms from home, then left
to their stiff-legged sleep.

All night the town is shrill with their troubled dreams
as they breathe the smells of their quarters,
recalling the pent-up days,
the galloping sea.

Efnysien, half-brother
of Brân and Branwen

And someone who hears these newcomers
calling across the darkness
in their raw voices

wonders why no one told him
his country had changed.

He is half a brother, which is no brother at all,
a splinter in the flesh of the family.
He is called Also and By The Way,
a man there's no space for in
a Snowdon of tent.

And his swan of a sister, who seems to walk
without moving her feet, nudged at times
to right and left by currents
only she can feel,

who shines with the weird light of a swan,
smiles at him vaguely as if
trying to place him –

to marry a foreign king,
and not ask his leave!

*Insulted, Efnysien
attacks Matholwch's
horses*

He's running through the town with a knife, from shriek to shriek.
The shrieks make him feel better. Most are not his.
The horses kick out sideways at him,
barge at him with their shoulders.
He's supple and quick.

He's carrying the branch of a horse's tail –
he can't remember which horse it's from –
surprised to find each one whole,
with its tail, eyes, lips,

and have to cut all over again.
He is unhorsing a king
one cut at a time,

till the red reaches the sky,
and his laughter stops.

Matholwch tries to flee

Most cumbersome of all the surreptitious noises:
a king packing to sneak away from his hosts.
They're hammering and heaving for hours,
the last few dozen people
he can rely on.

His horses have been insulted to the bone.
He has a stable of gargoyles now,
bloody-masked scarecrows of meat,
fit only for hounds.

The woman, at least, seems authentic,
and still has all her organs,
though little to say.

These people give with one hand,
slash with the other.

Brân will not let Matholwch leave, but gives him presents to compensate for the offence

Caught on the road. (His Grace regrets the kingdom is locked.)
They gauge the thickness of his little finger
for the silver rod they'll forge for him –
as tall as your esteemed self,
Measure of Brightness!

They beat a gold plate to the size of his face,
a small sun glowing through its bruises,
as if in cheery reproach
to his pewter gloom.

They're making the visitor they'd like,
a dazzle of countenance,
a stalk of body.

Brân refuses to punish Efnysien

The horses shall be replaced.
The brother must live.

[29]

Once more he's sitting in the bandaged air of the tent
beside his host's knees, staring into his cup,
where he sees only blood and himself.
The vast voice sounds from above:
What more can we give?

One final present, a
magic cauldron . . .

It's saying something about a cooking pot.
They're dragging it in, scoring the grass,
a crusted black iron vat
that could boil an ox.

Has someone struck it? The tent's ringing,
a note he feels in his teeth.
This is the cauldron

. . . that can resurrect
the dead

that simmers dead warriors
back to speechless life.

Branwen arrives in
Ireland

WHAT has the morning put on for the queen's arrival?
Chiffon, muslin, cotton and lace, white, white, white,
sky flouncing its hefty petticoats,
waves breaking in their new tops,
ships in their aprons.

What are the chores of this auspicious morning?
Lather, scour, rinse, hang out, work, work, work,
sea's suds, wind's scrub, clouds' boiling,
the ships' sheets straining.

How many of everything? Thirteen.
Thirteen waves doffing their caps,
bowing her to port,

thirteen sails to attend her,
luckiest of queens!

*Gwern, son of Branwen
and Matholwch*
She can feel the baby asleep in the other room,
a warm garment stowed in a chest till needed.
Soon it will be time to take him out –
the afternoon's shivering
with winter twilight,

and she goes to the window, knowing she'll see
the waves of cindery birds passing,
a flocking dark, like nightfall
or the thought of death.

*News of Efnysien's
crime reaches Ireland
and causes unrest*
Another demonstration today
against foreign influence.
She heard the shouting

and recognised the word *horse*.
She daren't go outside.

*Matholwch punishes
Branwen to appease the
protestors*
Goodbye to the moss-coloured and the topaz velvet,
the chest stuffed with the empty shapes of women,
to the cold embrace of the necklace
and the warm hands of the maid,
the same age as you.

Goodbye to the gruff adventures of the night,
and the man who startled you with them,
the fallen trees of his limbs,
on your way to sleep.

Goodbye, till the counsellors permit,
and the din at the gates fades,
to the royal child,

the summer grass of his hair,
his gasp of a smile.

Here, where they torture the dead bodies of animals
with their own hissing fat, on black contraptions
of iron rods and slow-turning wheels,
here in the incandescence
where dinners are forged,

the heat inside her cheeks meets the heat outside.
Shielding her face from the furnace glare,
she kneels at the sweaty trough
and wrings out the dough,

pummelling the damp weight in her chest.
She is no more than *that* now,
to be worked and slapped,

the air knuckled out of her –
a few pounds of soft.

Her heaven is cluttered with pans and strings of onions,
infested with feathery angels, the birds,
whose shadows no longer frighten her
as they crisscross the kitchen.
Her omens are spent.

This afternoon, a polished pip of an eye
round the corner of the kneading trough,
an adjustment of its head
to look at her face,

and the small being's next to her knee,
ignoring her now, intent
on its left shoulder,

where some stars have come adrift
in its midnight gown.

Branwen has trained
the starling to carry a
message

COACHED by three years of breadcrumb words, the starling
spirals towards the ground, a single snowflake
once part of a whirligig blizzard,
arcs through the tent's opening,
dances a high jig

Brân

in the stately air of the council chamber,
a fly tickling the king's oaken cheeks,
then settles on his shoulder,
hitching up its wings,

seemingly bothered by something there.
A thread is looped round each one,
trailing a white scroll

that the king removes and reads:
his sister's letter.

Farewell to Britain as
Brân invades Ireland
to avenge Branwen's
ill-treatment

Green island, grey island, purple island, mystified,
weepy island, constantly wetting the bed,
toddler swaddled in crumpled woollens,
itchy with rashes of trees,
the king must leave you

lullabied in the nursery of the ocean.
May no bad dreams come while he's away,
no thieves try the door handle,
no ghosts haunt your nights.

His men march to the side of the ships
in the whinny of trumpets,
and the king, hoicking

Brân carries the
musical instruments
for the army

a jangling sackful of harps,
steps into the sea.

A watchman on the
Irish coast

The work you do with your eyes isn't the easiest:
some blurry days when the sea's aching with tears,
he can't separate it from the sky,
with not a scratch of a mast
to fix his gaze on.

This morning, a grey fur, as if it's grown mould;
no amount of blinking will clear it.
It grows wider and taller,
black stems hung with threads.

Masts he can understand, but what's that
bobble in the midst of them
lurching and stopping,

then lurching again? A buoy?
A huge floating head?

No ship can carry Brân
so he walks across the
Irish Sea

Slithering on weedy rocks, he feels the sea's cold weight
push against his armour. Fingers of water
slip into gaps no arrow has found:
a fat bladder of ocean,
he rusts as he walks,

dragging the tingle of the harps behind him,
one arm fending off the banging ships,
crunching the crabs and lobsters,
gawped at by herring.

He rises at last, with waterfalls
springing out of his armpits,
and spits out the salt,

sodden colossus, never
to feel dry again.

The Liffey   Half god, half shire horse, he reaches the river. Beyond,
the Irish wait beneath their quivering spears.
He's heard there are lodestones on the bed
that can rip out a boat's nails,
and the bridge is down.

Brân acts as a bridge   So he kneels on the mud in front of his men
and stretches across. They furnish him
with a walkway of hurdles
that prickles his back,

then the boots start, every man treading
his weight into the taut spine,
till each one's printed

into the pith of his nerves:
battalions of pain.

Matholwch sends a   . . . not even the armies of water can hold him back.
letter suing for peace   Having regard to his wrath &c.,
and the regrettable besmirchment
of Her Grace our former queen,
now happily cleansed,

we hereby abdicate, our named successor,
Gwern   that child whose blood unites both the realms,
whose blank brow &c.
vouchsafes our candour . . .

The Irish will build   *Item*, a dwelling-place to be built
Brân a house   for him, who has never known
the calm of indoors,

so many by so many
cubits of sawn oak . . .

The half-brother's shown round the house, scattering footsteps
at the bottom of a canyon of echoes.
How can somewhere so new feel haunted?
The crossed shadows of pillars
trap him in their cage,

each one distorted by the knobbly outgrowth
of a leather sack hung from a peg.
It's flour, they tell him, to bake
loaves for the army.

He puts his hand inside, finds the head
of the swordsman hidden there,
grips it, and squeezes.

One hundred sacks, one hundred
heads crushed to slurry.

Gwern's coronation
takes place in the
new house

Crown him with the gold of the hearth, cense him with its smoke,
let the clatter of burning wood acclaim him.
Seat him on an inglenook of throne,
array him in orange light
in the fire's sanctum,

with armies flickering on each side of him
in the hot heart of his uncle's house,
tiny seed in the centre
of the sunflower!

Let his mother's face shine white on him
that was scorched red in the glare
of the cooking fire.

Soften the swords and spearpoints
to the glow of bronze.

He runs round the ring of light between the warlords' knees,
to be rumpled, smoothed, cherished, gloated over
or batted from one to another
in front of an audience
of yawning soldiers.

Just one place repels him, the draughty corner

Efnysien

where his half-uncle's sitting apart.
Called at last, he goes over,
and holds himself out

to the arms of his kinsman, who laughs
and lifts him above all heads,
then throws him lightly

headfirst into the coughing
red throat of the fire.

Gwern

One king is crawling in the fire, a lizard of flame
lost in a labyrinth of magma tunnels
and caves of dark heat, where daffodils
bloom with a sigh, and timbers
collapse on his back,

Brân

the other takes his sister under his arm,
as she burns in the boy's pain, her scream
fusing with his, and kicks out
to free her body,

clamped, like her son's, by a wooden weight.
Brân draws his girder of sword
as the Irish rise,

and shouts his challenge to them:
Hounds of Gwern, beware!

The two armies join
in battle in the giant's
house

The two armies push together, a battle indoors,
a covered marketplace of obscure shouting,
the sound of chopping in a forest
of regular, stunted trunks,
a crush of strangers,

too close for breathing, or, when you spin away
into the reach of the swinging swords,
a dance of the drunken knights
in their hacked armour.

Men fall like boys pretending to die,
and lie with their limbs askew
on the sticky floor.

The Irish are constantly
reinforced

Always the silent numbers
press into the hall.

Efnysien speaks to an
enemy warrior

Man with a broken tooth, panting against a pillar
in the ashlight, near the smashed moon of the fire,
twitching in your stupor, I have you,
my sword-point against your throat,
but you say nothing.

A battle's a living thing. It's resting now,
and only you and I are awake,
if you are. Your mouth's open
but no words come out.

What if I press harder, cut the words
out of your throat? Empty eyes,
a broken-toothed smile.

Dead warriors revived
by the magic cauldron
cannot speak

There's the long scar on your neck:
I killed you last night.

Outside the main door they're boiling soup. You can smell it
if you get close, a broth richer than chicken,
but with a sweet rustiness to it,
like the taste of your own blood
when you bite your tongue.

*Efnysien plays dead,
planning to destroy
the cauldron*

He lies with the Irish dead. Two men drag him
feet first into brightness, then stack him
in a larder of corpses
beside the cauldron.

Crushed by armour, his cheek pressed against
a man's torn belly, he hears
the heave-ho and splash

as the dead men are pitched in
to be boiled to life.

A moment in mid-air, the hot mists rising round him,
when it doesn't seem too late: the pull of down,
the one-after-another of time,
are rules he need not accept.
He's not yet falling,

then with a sort of snap his life shuts on him.
Liquid pain rises through his body,
till he's as big as the world.
He relearns his shape,

a map of purple and orange fire,
the ovals of his buttocks,
his nape's fierce island,

a scream that plunges inward
as he goes under.

Death is a brink inside him. He surges towards it
on the boiling current of his agony,
desiring only the rush and fall
to scatter him through the dark.
He doesn't reach it.

The heat grows bearable. He opens his eyes
on a scene occluded by bubbles,
the large ones gulping the small
as they storm upwards.

Dead warriors cuddle and nudge him,
gesturing with eely limbs,
opening fish mouths.

As their wounds fade to dull pink,
they strive to be born.

He sees himself running through the night, a horse's tail
absurdly in his hand. He feels a man's skull
crunching to pulp between his fingers,
sees a boy crawl in the fire
as if he lived there,

Efnysien's superhuman   his sister, clamped under a huge arm, screaming.
strength is increased by   The cauldron's power simmers in him,
the cauldron's power   no corpse but a living man,
with a giant's blood.

He stretches out to touch hot metal
with his hands and feet, pressing
against walls of pain,

Efnysien destroys the   till the cauldron's skull shatters
cauldron, and dies   and he is nothing.

The heat hits the air with a smack. Everything staggers.
The island's pots are broken into millions.
Men nearby are smashed; others are pierced
or scythed by wheeling splinters,
or drowned and scalded.

The regurgitated army of the dead
crawls in its sleep on the steaming grass,
grey crabs that fumble out of
the unrolling tide.

They are fumbling, too, inside the house,
the few who can move at all,
in the squeezed darkness

between the heaped-up earthworks
whose turves were once men.

The nettle-sting of a spear in the king's foot lengthens
and branches into threads of acid. His heart
knows what this means before his mind does:
an unlatched door in the wind,
it bangs at his frame.

A tree of poison is growing inside him.
He crouches far away watching it
and the dying of the man
he thought was himself:

how the bucking colt of his body
still tugs against the halter,
even as it dies.

A strange creature – he wishes
he'd known it better.

His head still lives. He calls the last seven of his men
and tells them to take his sword and cut it off.
They see the dried canals of wrinkles
on his cheeks, the chapped flagstones
of skin on his lips –

saddest of all, the liquid globes of his eyes,
shining like bogwater, delicate
even in this roughcast face.
He is all his men,

The men must take the head to London to be buried
the size each one is in his own mind.
Their last mission's a journey
and a burial.

It takes the men all their strength
to pick up the sword.

Branwen; Aber Alaw in Anglesey
SHE can see both islands from here: the green and grey one
she is at last standing on; the streak of woad
that might be a top layer of sea
or underlining of sky.
She should be queen there,

if there is anyone still alive in it.
The many blues between are gentler,
an empire awash with tears
and peopled by fish.

Branwen dies of grief
There's nothing to hold her but the earth
so she lies down and hugs it
till she feels it plunge

into the deepest blue of them all
where no one can live.

They have woven a wicker basket for the king's head.
In the golden gloom of its silk canopy
it dozes on dozens of cushions,
but only closes its eyes
in waking moments,

when it seems to be looking inside itself
at the everywhere of its body,
then answers all their questions
in a voiceless sigh.

It tells them to bury its sister
where she can look at Ireland
from the riverbank,

which they do, trusting it knows
what the dead can see.

Crossing the island with the head asleep on a cart,
they learn the tinctures of mud: brown, russet, white,
a watery black that sprays and sets,
and a bilious ochre
that clutches the wheels.

They've only known the top few inches of land.
It's deep, and loves them glutinously.
They sense its puddingy dark
under hoofs and feet.

The head is there most of the time now.
They can hear it muttering
to some unseen friends.

The air is too harsh for it.
It wants the moist earth.

London

Here is the city that keeps an eye on the sunrise,
where there is always a scattering of masts
on the gleaming slug of a river
that oozes east to the sea
and everywhere else.

The head can see the world from here, in the hill

*Tower Hill; the head
will watch over the
kingdom*

called the White Mound. They cover its eyes
with the soil's crumbly blindfold:
the light will reach them.

Sunken brain of the city, feeling
all its footsteps and voices
with whiskers of nerves,

guard our island from swordsmen
and their stabbing ships!

The Tale of the Fog and the Fieldmouse

A ND now it's afterwards, the head in its mound of earth,
straining its eyes, sun gloating on the river,
a wind blowing from everywhere else,

The seven who brought
Brân's head to London

and seven men shaking hands,
muttering goodbyes,

Pryderi (see the First
Branch)

till there are two left: one, the Prince of the West
we once saw riding a stripling horse,
the child dropped on the threshold
by a severed claw;

Manawydan, brother
of Brân, who no longer
has a realm, as another
lord has seized the
throne during the war
in Ireland

the other, a prince of nowhere now,
his closest kin the great head
they must leave behind;

both stranded in afterwards,
in the gooseflesh wind.

Dyfed, Pryderi's
princedom in
west Wales

They ride back to the country of coppery sunsets,
its fields cut off by the blue ditch of the sea
and its days cut off by the sodden
amnesia of sea mist,
a half-real domain,

Cigfa, wife of Pryderi;
Rhiannon, his mother

where the two women smiling in the doorway,
all air and light, like unfurled beech leaves,
didn't sprout from the same tree
on the same morning.

Rhiannon

One of them we saw from a hilltop
riding along a white road
following the sun.

She is still not out of breath
these hot miles later.

This is all her work, this embroidery of torchlight,
music and smoke, of benches, tables, rafters,
cups, plates and faces. They stretch and shine
with the faint shrilling of thread
as she draws them out.

Manawydan falls in
love with Rhiannon

Or that's how it seems to the man beside her,
in the blur of wine and exhaustion,
watching the way her fingers
weave air as she talks.

The mother of his friend . . . He knows now
that there's no such thing as time.
He can still that hand

in the leather of his own
and the world won't move.

Deer flicker in the forests. The days chase after them.
And the rivers bring forth fish after their kind,
the slow brown ones shadowy with trout,
and the glassy mountain streams
twisting with salmon.

And the fields are complicated with flowers,
summer an insurrection of bees,
the days like clover petals'
pinpricks of nectar.

They ride between one hall and the next,
sending the servants in front
with the cooking pots.

Their empire is everywhere,
their realm, each other.

Gorsedd Arberth,
the hill of visions

This is the hub, the green knoll in the midst of the green
where a prince sat and watched a woman riding.
The court sits on the cushiony turf:
the two lords and their ladies,
their roost of nobles,

all still, though their garments shiver in the wind,
the landscape's hoarse silence in their ears,
watching the dumbshow of clouds,
the fiddling cornfields.

A magic fog descends

Then there's nothing to see but whiteness.
A chilly linen of fog
clings to their faces,

and the air rings like a pan
clanging on granite.

They are limbless and bodiless. There is no beyond.
They press against the clammy wall of the self
that pulses in time to their breathing,
the otherness of the world
at last swept away:

there is only you, as you have always known,
and when a thinness insinuates,
when space and colour leak back,
the brightness is sham.

Two couples stand on the blowing tump,
but where the nobles roosted
is grass and thistles.

No corn gilds the fields, no sheep
mooch on the hillsides.

The country has been enchanted

All that we laid on the land – the long grasses we sowed
for the goodness in the seeds, the animals
that chewed the country into tameness,
the dwellings of wood and stone –
the fog has lifted.

Only these four are left, and their four horses.
They ride back through the unhedged acres
in an unfamiliar dusk
without smoke or lights.

The hall's still there, a hulk, black on grey,
bigger than they remembered.
How did they live here

in this quarry of footsteps,
this towering night?

The memory of fire, a rose-grey tinge to the dark.
It was never allowed to go out. Dig down
through softs and cools, past flaky charcoals,
to where a red star's dying.
Coax it with splinters,

build it a shelter out of twigs and pinecones.
It trembles in the black, starts to shrink.
Feed it whatever stars eat
till it flares yellow.

Cosset that larval flame as it grows
and breeds hungry butterflies
that twitch on the logs,

till you can see each other
in your tent of light.

Without servants or
courtiers, the two
couples must look after
themselves

There is a larder all round them, the dead animals
they were to feast on: gold eyes in the firelight,
a table laden with butchered limbs
and fuzzy hummocks of fur
blotted with bloodstains.

From now on they are living with the absent,
the hundredweight of its appetite
and its spidering shadows
upflung on the walls.

The women hack the fur from a hare
till it's naked and gleaming,
skewered on a sword.

They season their loneliness
with smoke and burnt meat.

Their world has been taken, but they still have their country.
The men ride over sheepless hills with the dogs
squirming and seething around the hoofs,
and the deer sift through the trees
as they did before.

In the kitchen the women manhandle pots
that gong against the hard surfaces,
always outnumbered by meat
with its blood-rimmed eyes.

In lonely moments, the air's as vast
as the stillness of a church
that sees and hears you.

They don't fear the emptiness,
but what might live there.

They can survive on venison, salmon and honey.
They can brush their own horses, feed their own dogs.
They know the old stories, the old songs.
Each has another's body
to feel for at night.

They miss strangers: light through a half-open door
and people talking in a cottage
who'll never know you are there
but who might be you,

that feeling, just as you fall asleep,
that your mind's plunging into
a sea of sleepers.

If there are still people left,
they have to find them.

They go to England   THIS is a peopled country: the woods smell of sawdust.
          Each farm's announced by the barking of its dogs
and the throaty chortle of a cock
celebrating a morning
that lasts till sunset.

Hereford   The grey crust of a town wall, shaggy with weeds.
The gate is open. They pass beneath
a pigeon-ruffled darkness
to crowded daylight,

all hoofs and wheels, shoulders and shouting.
They are unknown in this place
of mongers and wrights –

exotic beings, gaudy
as beasts on a shield.

They learn a trade . . .　　They've grown used to the dinginess, the scent of leather.
The hand finds its way among the laid-out tools
to the pricking iron or edge shave,
the awl, the punching mallet
or the half-moon knife.

And the mind's humming its tune: tack the webbing
to the wooden tree, strain the linen,
stuff it with wool and block it,
nail on the calfskin.

. . . making saddles　　They've sat in the saddle; now they know
how to make flaps and cantles,
girths and surcingles.

The blue glaze on the pommel
is their royal touch.

They are the lords of saddlery now. Every pommel
in Hereford's enamelled with their azure,
while their rivals brood in the workshops
among heaps of unsold tack,
sharpening half-moons.

Jealous competitors　　A boy with a message: they're coming for you.
The aproned men smelling of leather
have creaked out of the buff gloom
to lurch down the street.

They're outside now, swinging their mallets.
Listen, and you'll hear the snip
of bulldog pliers.

So, do you fight, or slip out
the tradesmen's entrance?

Another trade:
shield-making

Shrewsbury

What is a shield but a saddle strapped to the forearm,
wood and leather? Most of the tools are the same.
They cut, glue, tack and paint, while outside
the wheels of another town
grind the street to flour.

Their azure has the glassy sheen of before,
but now they have learned other tinctures,
stains, metals, furs. Knights trust them
with their ancestry.

No quarterings are too intricate.
They paint bendlets, nebuly,
lozenges, chevrons.

Zigzags of argent and or
glimmer on the walls.

The shieldmakers are rampant. You can hear them outside
clacking their steel against the limewood blanks.
Warriors would fight; tradesmen must leave.
The rows of emblazoned shields
must fend for themselves.

Shoemaking in Ludlow

A shoe's a shield for the foot. Another town.
The red warmth of Cordovan leather
and a shop clunky with lasts
like maimed wooden feet.

The cordwainers rise from their benches,
picking up their skivving knives,
trenchets and gouges.

Town is no place for you; trade's
an edgy business.

Dyfed

THE land managed without them. Woodpeckers ratcheted,
a beetle cantilevered from a soft log,
spangled flies twitched between slants of sun
that tiptoed across the ground,
marking the non-hours.

Only the dogs, curled in their village of smells,
remembered, or sensed something missing,
a taller companionship
that troubled the brain.

The four return home

Now the old noises are back: clopping,
the chink of metal, the brisk
bafflement of words,

and their barks rise in response,
and their tails whiplash.

The men go hunting . . .

There's no white in the woods except the trunks of birches
with their bleak radiance, like knobbly moonbeams.
The rest is greens and browns. What moves here
is half dissolved, a nuance
of bark and dead leaf.

*. . . and chase a
white boar*

So what's the white that bursts from a spume of leaves,
gleaming and bare, a hefty Venus,
and stands there, steaming at them,
with its smirking tusks?

The dogs have seen a ghost. They shrink back
as it shakes its mythic head
and minces away,

with a tweak of its pert tail,
a flash of buttocks.

It is distant and close: a blob of white in the trees,
a scrabbling in the bushes, an inward snort
as of a creature inhaling earth.
The dogs half-bay, half-whimper,
and cringe as they run.

It is as if the forest opens for them,
and somehow a castle has happened
where nothing should be, its walls
a grin of marble.

The boar's expected. It trots across
and vanishes through the gate,
the dogs following.

The hunters watch. No armed men
hail them from the walls.

Pryderi

Still the boy who thinks with his legs, the Prince of the West
won't leave his dogs trapped in that mausoleum.
His friend calls from the edge of the woods
as he crosses the clearing
towards the white mouth.

Inside's a courtyard paved with egg-shaped cobbles.
He's slipping on their shine as he walks
through an abstract space, without
people or buildings,

just a well, and a bowl of chased gold
hanging above it on chains
that stretch to the sky.

He is caught in
a magic trap

It sings, though no wind stirs it,
and he reaches out.

Manawydan returns alone
Evening the colour of smoke, smoke smelling of autumn,
a man on a horse, a horse without a man,
and a dogless silence all round them:
a cold draught of absence blows
through this homecoming.

Rhiannon goes to find her son
It's the mother who rides out, finding her way
on the hills by the sky's remnant light,
and through the woods by the give
of twigs and brambles.

The castle has a light of its own.
The bowl hangs in the courtyard
like a metal moon,

with the statue of her son
joined by one finger.

Someone is calling his name in a long-ago voice.
There is a slither of footsteps behind him.
He waits, as he has all afternoon,
right knee bent, weight poised over
the ball of his foot.

His finger thrums with the singing of the bowl.
He feels his heart still stumbling inside,
the flutter of breath he can't
wrangle into words.

She puts him to one side of her mind:
she has to touch that chill fire
with its web of lines.

Rhiannon is also caught
Its stillness jolts through her arm,
and a loud mist falls.

*Manawydan and Cigfa
are alone together*

THE hall is deep. They sit at the table and look up
at the silt of shadows that obscures the roof.
The two of them might be pond insects
balanced on their tense circles
on the water's skin:

an upside-down thought that he can't break out of.
A dropped word would dispel the silence,
but he can't think of any.
She won't meet his eye.

From now on they will have to forget
that they're those straggly creatures
called man and woman.

They are the two caretakers
of a loneliness.

*Manawydan turns
to farming*

He has hunted, wrought, traded. Now he has wheat to sow.
They'll regrow the land on their own, field by field.
He digs his hand into gritty seed
that lodges under his nails,
pellets of being,

then casts it from him to flitter in the wind
and find a purchase in the furrows
he has scratched with a forked branch
across their acres.

This is their investment in weather.
Sun and rain mean something now,
though they aren't sure what.

Under the soil, white feelers
are groping for light.

Every day he studies the three fields he has planted
till he knows each shucked-off snailshell and wormcast.
Perhaps the earth is spent. Nothing stirs
on the inscrutable black
but birds and beetles.

Then there's nothing to see for a week but rain
that splatters in the yard. When it stops,
the claggy fields are covered
in a mist of green.

Much of it is weeds, but the small spines
in their regimented rows
are starting to push,

the points of their lances massed
at the dark border.

By now it has grown so tall they can hear its swishing
as they lie in their beds. The land has changed shape,
a ghostly presence outside, shifting
yet rooted, as if the wind
has been planted there.

The stalks are coarsening, the narrow leaves catch
any sun there may be, and wither.
The fields warm to the colour
of a lion's pelt.

He thinks of all the blades he's sharpened.
Tonight he'll use his whetstone
on a reaping hook.

The starchy grass is bowing
its thousands of heads.

As he approaches the field this wheat-coloured morning,
the sound is wrong, a dry ticking, not a rush.
It looks ragged: overgrown stubble
scratching at the air, each stalk
cut off at the neck.

His first field has been ruined . . .

He spends the morning in that prickly ocean,
trying to glean in its golden depths.
Whatever ripped through here took
all but a few grains.

At last he looks up. The second field
the other side of the hedge
is ripe and intact.

. . . as has his second field

Next day he returns to find
another maimed crop.

Now, as he stands at the edge of his beheaded field,
the sky pressing upon him like a headache,
the air stiffening to a jelly,
his mind is trying to run,
but his limbs won't move.

He feels the presence of someone watching him,
an engineer of fog and clamour,
sweeper-away of harvests,
livestock and people.

And there's the third field, nodding at him.
Red butterflies of poppies
twitch among the stems.

This time he won't be swindled.
Tonight he'll wait up.

A summery night, with a curds-and-whey moon rising.
He leans against a bank, watching the stems stir.
Nothing happens, again and again,
in that land of verticals
and leggy shadows.

He has been listening, without knowing it,
to a sound he's never heard before –
an intricate pittering
like granular rain.

When he looks round, the grass is swarming
with something soft that has eyes
and hillocks of backs.

High tide in the reeling corn

A plague of mice   as the mice sweep in.

The stems are plump with them, swollen fruit, fuzzy tumours,
uncountable as the wheat they clamber up,
no longer than the heads they crouch on
to gnaw at the neck, then drop
lightly as acorns.

They surge both ways now, the returners bearing
a plumed trophy of seedhead aloft.
They hardly squirm underfoot
as he tramples through.

He's flailing in the stilted dimness
at the shapes tickling round him,
but they won't be caught,

*He catches one of
the mice*   except for one fat sluggard
he puts in his glove.

For the mouse in the glove, it's a warm and padded night,
with long fingers of void to lose its tail in.
Sometimes it panics, remembering
the coolness of naked air
on limbs free to run.

But this leather universe seems to love it
in a stifling way. There's room to sleep.
She is female. In her womb
more captives are curled.

Rhiannon and Pryderi
have been imprisoned
by their magical enemy

Elsewhere, in a prison made of stone,
where strands of fog still linger,
a mother and son,

clanking weights hung round their necks,
squat in the damp straw.

Cigfa asks Manawydan
about the mouse

The hangman in her chamber strings his glove on a peg,
and whose is the plump hand that wriggles inside?
I hang a thief's hand here, my lady.
When daylight blanches the hill
I'll hang it for good.

She sees two pinhead eyes in the glove's dark mouth.
Its cry is a pinscratch in her head.
A spiderweb whisker shines
in the candlelight.

What tree is stunted enough to hang
so small a thief? What fine rope
can it dangle from?

How will the noose find lodging
where there is no neck?

Manawydan sets out
to hang the mouse on
Gorsedd Arberth

The knoll is blacker than the fields, a burnt-out bonfire,
as he climbs, the fat glove swinging from his hand,
His feet know the textures of his way:
gulp, crumble, slither and snag.
He senses the top,

the centre of an invisible circle,
as the dark acres crowd round to watch,
feels in his bag for two forks
and a ball of string,

and sets up his puppetshow gibbet:
fork-hilts pushed into the turf,
a stick between them.

A gowned man is approaching
as the day whitens.

The first stranger he's seen here since the day of the fog,
almost as tattered as the dawn's purple clouds,
and much less showy, this sandalled monk
with blood crusting his toenails
and a tramp's hobble.

The monk bargains for
the mouse's life

– Lord, whose is that sharp face peering from your hand?
– A thief I caught stealing from my fields.
– And that gimcrack contraption?
– My mousetrap gallows.

– Lord, here's the gold coin I got as alms.
Rather than see the mouse hang,
I'll buy it from you.

The hangman is resolute
and the monk limps off.

And now a priest appears against the sky's rose window,
declaiming from the pulpit of his saddle.
His offer is three gold coins to save

Manawydan refuses
the priest's offer

this furry snippet of life.
My lord knows better,

and as the priest rides off, the horizon burns
with a sunrise of a procession,
the chanting and jingling train
of some potentate.

Mounted knights, choristers, monks and priests,
wind past the foot of the hill,
wreathed in incense fumes.

Then, from a curtained litter,
a hand's raised to bless.

The bishop is the
enchanter Llwyd in
disguise

A bishop in full panoply, crozier, mitre,
lifting his skirts free of the mud as he climbs,
till he stands panting on the summit,
pulling the mist around him,
as he makes his bid.

Seven gold coins for its life. No, twenty-four.
The train of baggage you see down there,
my horses, soldiers, servants,
for one pregnant mouse.

Manawydan considers
his offer

He weighs the life twisting in his hand,
a drachm or so of creature,
some scruples of young,

against those bluish cohorts
steaming below them.

Here is my price: my wife and my friend. – You shall have them.
– And the world they belonged to: cornfields, cattle,
villages, farms. – You shall have those, too.
– Now tell me who the mouse is,
and why you want her.

*Llwyd seeks vengeance
for the devastation of
Ireland (see the Second
Branch)*

The bishop laughs. – And you never stole a world?
You left an island smothered in ash.
My methods are more subtle:
I think things away.

I set the army of mice on you
with my wife as its general.
That's her in your hand,

with my children inside her.
Let us make peace now.

– One more thing. Protect this western land from enchantments,
so no one can steal it. The war is over:
let this spell be the last. No revenge
on me, my friends or people.
– All this you shall have.

*Lwyd's pregnant wife
is returned to human
form*

He puts down the mouse and the bishop taps it
with the butt of his staff. A woman
rises through the mist, naked
and pumpkin-bellied.

*Rhiannon and Pryderi
are released and the
spell is lifted*

And here, crouching, the mother and son,
rubbing the red on their necks
where the weights were hung.

And when the mist clears, the hills
are puffballed with sheep.

THE FOURTH BRANCH

The Tale of the Pigs and the Flower-Woman

Aftermath the feast, it is good for the great one to rest
with his feet in the lap of the footholder,
who must scratch wherever he itches,
while a man strumming a harp
turns him into song.

His light fills the hall, his wine flushes the cheeks
of the listeners at the tables.
His deeds flicker round the walls
till he feels dizzy.

Gwydion

Then it is good to hear the stranger
who rode to the castle gate
with night just behind,

and is twitching like someone
with stories to tell.

He is short, narrow-shouldered, with a cottongrass beard
and the pinched face of a frog, the eyes swollen,
and when he speaks, in his jackdaw voice,
he puts his head on one side,
to see what he's said,

its shadow flitting over people's faces.
He is the world's best storyteller,
so he says; that is, he's lived
through its best stories.

They watch him rummage inside himself
for the tales he carries round
to pay for his meals,

till, with a sigh, he finds one
to put before them.

Gwydion begins
his story
There are the bones of a story in tonight's dinner.
He looks across the table at the carcass,
a wrecked cathedral of curving ribs,
the platter strewn with white flesh
and scraps of crackling.

Annwfn
You know the pig is a creature of Unland.
Set one loose in the autumn forest
and watch it snuffle the ground
in search of its home.

Tonight we've dined on the rind and fat
and tissue of fairy meat.
There were no pigs here

Pwyll
Arawn
before the Prince of the West
swapped with his double.

He spent a year in the country beyond the forest,
chief of Wherever and its wispy people,
See the First Branch
killed their enemy at the brown ford,
and came back the blood brother
of a bloodless king.

They sent each other presents: horses, hawks, hounds,
and, one year, a herd of animals
with small eyes, harrumphing speech
and babyish smiles.

By now the prince had died, as happens
Pryderi
on our side of the forest.
His son received them

after he'd got back the land
See the Third Branch
that was thought away.

Gwydion tells how he tricked Pryderi into giving him the pigs . . .

Pig-daydreams squealed in my mind as I rode to the court,
taking only the stories I stood up in
and a saddlebag full of mushrooms.
I sat with the prince, and talked
his fire to ashes,

. . . using magic to create an irresistible present

till he would give me anything but his pigs.
They were not to be had for stories.
I went back to my mushrooms
and laboured all day,

and returned to him with twelve stallions,
shiny as polished bog-oak,
twelve hounds blazed with white,

with jewelled collars and leashes,
and twelve golden shields.

The flight of Gwydion and the pigs is commemorated in place-names . . .

There was no time to lose. The pigs scuttled before me,
snouts grazing the earth, pink earthworm tails writhing,
through pasture and wood to the high moor.
Trotters scratched scree as they ran
over the grey tops.

They left their dung and the names of villages:

. . . Mochdref; Mochdref; Mochnant; Mochdref; Creuwrion

we passed Pigton; then on through Swineville,
Hogwater, Ham Porcorum,
and reached Styhaven,

The magic wears off

as the prince watched his new horses sag
to slimy fungus, his dogs
to heaps of toadstools,

as he mustered his armies
and marched after us.

Gwydion pauses in
his storytelling

Hᴇ glances at the footholder, who's gently rocking
the feet in her lap like two callused babies.
Is that half-smile on her face for him?
A murmur goes round the hall.
Pigs? Why not dragons?

Is this a fitting subject for a story?
He feels them twisting under his words,
and struggles to control them.
Certainly not pigs –

that was by way of a preamble.
This is a story about
(that half-smile again)

a lady whose noble charge
was a great man's feet.

Math, ruler
of Gwynedd

The feet were my uncle's. He is the Lord of the North.
No doings between a man and a woman
can be so nakedly chaste as this
cushioning of lower parts
before the world's eyes,

so her virginity goes without saying.

Aranrhod

My sister was the lord's footholder,
and carried herself like one
whose lap had been blessed.

Who knows a woman like her brother,
who's followed her through the court
to the dark garden,

and heard her breathy laughter,
so much like his own?

*Gwydion uses magic
to prove Aranrhod
is not a virgin, and
therefore not a suitable
footholder*

Had it gone without saying? It shouldn't be too hard
for one who can shape animals from mushrooms
to find what goes into a woman.
I cut a stick in the woods
and peeled a green wand,

then waited behind the door as she passed through
into the din of the hall, holding
the wand before her ankles
as if to trip her.

She saw it in time and skipped,
as a satin disturbance
shook her lifted skirts,

and something dropped to the floor
with a piglike squeal.

She put her hand between her legs as if to catch it,
then up to her mouth as if what she had dropped
had been no more than an ill-judged word,
then made as if to walk on,
till the room stopped her

with a red-hot silence she couldn't pass through,
though I saw her push at the taut air.
Something had been left open
that should have been sealed,

and the wand knew it. Now the court knew,
though they could not have said how.
She ran from the hall,

and I left with a bundle
wrapped up in my cloak.

Not knowing what to do with the bundle, I shut it
in the linen-chest at the foot of my bed.

Caer Aranrhod

My sister had fled to her castle
encrusted on the granite
by a sulky sea.

I was woken by a dawn chorus of one
that seemed to have got inside the room.
I leapt from my dream, flailing
at flying bagpipes –

there was nothing in the air but noise,
which came from the linen-chest.
I lifted the lid,

*The magic bundle is
Aranrhod's son*

and found a long-limbed baby
tangled in the folds.

I picked it up as if it had been real bagpipes,
wary of all those writhing appendages
that kept attaching themselves to me.
The body seemed plump with air
for all its wailing.

Only a woman would know how to work this.
Perhaps I'd broken it already:
its wet eyes goggled at me
as if to say so.

I pushed through the crowded court, coughing
to hide the noises which came
from my leather bag,

and sneaked into the village
to find a wet nurse.

Gwydion adopts
his nephew

PIGS are not fitting for stories – is a man better?
  For I saw there were the makings of a man
in that object. Soon he'd learned to walk,
and followed me round the court.
He had no name yet,

not having done anything to deserve one,
except sit on the beach and throw stones,
his fair hair catching the sun
like a glint of quartz.

His pebbles clonked on driftwood targets
and rattled into shingle
for whole afternoons.

You might have called it aimless,
but it wasn't that.

There was no place for a mother in his stony life,
but I knew a child was supposed to have one,
and he would drift anywhere I asked.

They visit Caer
Aranrhod

We found her among her knights,
a woman grandee.

The two looked at each other. I expected
hugs, tears, a confusion of softness,
and stood back to wait for it,
but no flurry came.

They turned to me, then, and I explained:
this was the boy she'd let slip
at our uncle's court.

I'd brought her leavings to her
and called them a son.

*Aranrhod disowns her
son and puts a curse
on him*

He was nobody before. When he left the castle
he was less than that. Instead of a mother,
he'd gained a mother's tug and pressure.
He would never have a name
until she named him.

If he felt any of this, he didn't say.
I had to do the feeling for him,
resting my hand on his blond
pebble of a head.

I could make animals from mushrooms.
I'd make a man out of this
small foreign body.

Next day we walked on the beach
and gathered seaweed.

Pods, stragglers, feelers, the sea's green and russet flora
slimed on the rocks, or was baked to a crackle,
a tatterdemalion harvest,
rich with a leathery stink
like last year's stockfish.

On the wet plain of sand below the shingle,
we piled an oval of bladderwrack,
swathed it in mud-coloured kelp
to form a ship's hull.

Dulse and laver for the deck, the mast
a spike of sea-grass flaunting
a sea-lettuce sail.

We stood on the squelchy deck
as the tide swam in.

We sidled along the coast on our ship of seaweed
that my imagination kept from sinking
and came to anchor below the rock
and its barnacle castle
where my sister was.

Knowing what went into her, and what came out,
I guessed what would draw her from her shell.
Even through rock she could sense
a new pair of shoes.

So we sat crosslegged on the deck
crafting vessels for her feet
from festoons of kelp,

till she arrived on the shore,
scenting sweet leather.

Gwydion and the boy   She saw a ship of oak and canvas, webbed with rigging,
are magically disguised   and boarded her. A man and boy at her feet,
the crew, sat in a jumble of shoes.
Their faces when they looked up
were vague and floaty.

Then came the wrangling of calfskin and money,
the prod and pinch of trying them on,
stroking of buckle and stitch,
the preen up and down.

She saw the boy's eyes lift from her feet
to a wren on the ship's rail.
He groped for a shell,

and threw with a flick, hitting
a needle-thin leg.

The wren was a confection of my own (Irish moss),
and it was I who placed the shell by his hand.

Aranrhod is tricked into giving her son a name

She laughed, then just as I'd known she would,
calling him butterhaired boy
and cleverfingers.

Lleu Llaw Gyffes

The name would do: Butterhair Cleverfingers.
As the ship foundered into seaweed
and we scrambled for the rock,
I told her as much.

Kelp-draped in her brine-sodden velvet,
she lay on the shore, gasping
like a beached mermaid.

She curses him a second time

He would never have weapons
except from her hands.

Lleu sulks because he cannot become a warrior

All knuckles and wristbones, he slept late to spite the sun.
He never tidied the strawyard of his face.
He shrugged as he walked, as if the world
felt slightly too small for him,
could ride any horse,

but still preferred to throw stones on the beach,
whose grinding greyness suited his mood:
half-mourning for a future
that might not happen.

They were his only weapons, too small
to kill anything fiercer
than an angry gull.

Time to ride to the castle,
wearing new faces.

They return, disguised,
to Caer Aranrhod and
are received as guests

Rearranging my stories so she didn't know them,
I talked us into dinner and right through it.
We went to our room high in the rock,
and the boy growled in his sleep
while I stretched my mind

The castle is
under attack

into the darknesses round us. At daybreak,
we heard the squirming cry of trumpets,
armed men clanking on the stairs,
volleys of knocking.

We stood at the slot of the window
and saw the sea white with sails,
sun stinging armour,

as the boats pressed through the waves
and men vaulted out.

Aranrhod asks her
guests for help, and
gives them weapons

She stood in the doorway. Every man would be needed,
even a storyteller. Even his boy.
The swords smelt sweetly of linseed oil
as she held them out to us.
We'd need spears as well.

The boy had disembowelled the air with one slice.
He rested the sword against the wall,
and took the spear, his arm raised
in a bird's-wing arc.

Here was a roost of arrows, nestling
wingtip to wingtip, a bow
that twanged like a lute.

Now he'd demolish the walls
to get at the sky.

*Gwydion's magic has
tricked her again*

Something was seeping into the room from the window.
She shook her head, listening. It was silence.
The only sound outside was the sea.
I led her over to look
at its blue cohorts.

Seagulls and oystercatchers whirled above it
for sails and flags; the wind carried off
any trumpet calls they made.
I felt my face change.

By that time she had guessed who we were,
and knew her son was gloating
over his weapons,

*She issues her
third curse*

but no woman born on earth
would be that boy's wife.

This time we couldn't trick her. All women were ruled out.
I had never noticed how many there were:
I felt their presence now, the moments
out walking or at table,
when he'd pause mid-word

at the mulch-dark eyes of a girl in the field,
or gaze at the soft sward of a dress,
like a rider surveying
its swells and valleys.

They'd found him too, his hair and cheekbones,
the limbs he stretched out as if
not sure they were his.

Our days were tense with looking
and looking away.

Meadowsweet for sweetness, with its smell of stale candy,
shrivelled cream flowers they strew between bedsheets;
broomflowers for silken gaudiness;
oak catkins for their gentle
tickling of the wind.

I, who had sculpted mushrooms, woven seaweed,
and whisked a fleet from feathers and spray,
could conjure what he needed
from these fripperies.

The air was golden with her pollen
as I heaped her on the bed
in frilly armfuls,

till a million petals fused
into a woman.

Blodeuedd

D ID she remember as she sat at her tapestry
stitching its marginalia of flowers,
or when she squeezed in between her sheets
and a scent of meadowsweet
haunted the darkness,

or when she rode over her husband's acres
just after the oak-leaves had opened,
bright with the greeny-yellow
of hearts of lettuce,

a time when she dangled in the wind,
when her insides were offered
to a nuzzling bee,

when she was part of it all,
when she was many?

She was the wife I had made for the man I had grown.
He rode, ruled, hunted, like any other lord,
while she sewed herself into silence,

Mur Castell those chilly castle evenings
when he was away.

A strangled bleat of horns from the distant woods.
Knowing it wasn't him, she listened,
willing it back when it died,
all one afternoon,

till she felt the hoofbeats in her chest.
At last the yapping went up
for a sunset kill,

and she called a servant to ride
and see who was there.

Gronw At the red hour when he was elbow-deep in entrails,
a man came to lead him out of the forest,
and he, stupid with blood and riding,
thought he had done something wrong,
when he hadn't yet.

Blodeuedd entertains A fire yellow as broom was lit in the hall.
him at the castle The water they brought him to wash in
had flowers floating in it,
and a stale-sweet smell,

but that was all round him, as if the air
had been shut in a clothes chest
full of potpourri.

The lady who greeted him
was honeyed with it.

They fall in love

As he was following her up the shadowy stairs
he tried to remember the moment he'd known.
Was there a hastily swallowed laugh,
a gaze she couldn't put down?
He could find nothing,

no brink he'd stepped over into dizziness,
unless the whole evening was a brink.
He couldn't picture her face,
only the candles

burning all round them, their beeswax smell
mingling with her candy scent.
They were lovers then,

and they would be lovers soon,
whoever she was.

*Gwydion has woven
magic spells to protect
Lleu's life; he can
only be killed in the
most improbable
circumstances . . .*

M Y nephew couldn't be killed like anyone's nephew.
His birth had been unlikely; I'd spent evenings
making his death unlikelier still,
knitting an invisible
chainmail of logic.

The spear would take a year of Sundays to forge,
hammering on the peaceful mornings
when everyone was in church.
Suppose you'd done so,

you'd need to find a way to kill him
neither indoors nor outdoors,
on foot nor horseback.

Well then, she asked her husband,
how can you be killed?

The Sunday bells and hymns hid the sound of hammering,
and she was working too, unpicking the snarl
I'd tangled around her husband's life.
Surely his wife should be told,
to keep him from harm?

. . . which Blodeuedd
tricks him into
revealing

Neither indoors not outdoors: in a bath-house
such as they build on the river bank
with a thatched roof but no walls,
so the wind blows through,

fanning the bather to goosepimples,
as he climbs out of the tub
between wet and dry.

It was hard to imagine –
she would build him one.

Gronw murders
Lleu . . .

In a house filled with wind, in a box filled with water
a man was singing himself clean. When he rose,
here was his wife leading a creature
that was half-sheep and half-deer
for him to climb on.

And there his killer found him, half-wet, half-dry,
with one foot on a goat's hairy back.
Just as I'd dreamed it, he died
of unlikeliness –

or didn't. As the spear broke his ribs
and spread its slick of poison
through his heart's flanges,

. . . but his spirit
escapes in the form
of an eagle, through
Gwydion's magic

something flew out with a scream,
flailing its feathers.

A MILE from the village, I could smell dung on the wind
and here was the first sow, trotting up the road
at the head of her file of piglets.
There were more pigs than people
in Styhaven now.

They snorted in the mud by the market cross,
smiling in their dreamy Unland way,
as I put my old question
to the villagers.

No one had seen a ragged eagle
that cried in a human voice,
except one old man,

who said his sow might show me
if I followed her.

At daybreak he unlatched the pen. The sky was mottled
with pinks, greys and whites like the back of the pig
that led me along the brambly path,
passing up acorns and slugs,
to a greendark cwm.

Here, among rocks furnished with moss, and tree-trunks
hung with loops of its mouldy knitting,
she'd found something white to eat;
blobs and flakes of it

fell in a sort of sleet from an oak.
The blobs were maggots, the flakes,
dead peelings of skin.

Up there was the mangy bird
I had come to catch.

It took all morning to talk him down: he'd forgotten
most of his humanness, and looked down at me
with one unfeeling globule of eye.
Murder meant nothing to him
and neither did love.

But when I sang he cried in his baby voice
as if he remembered the uncle
who'd dreamed up this feathered craft
where his soul now perched,

and fluttered downward from branch to branch,
to rest on the valley floor
where my wand could reach,

Lleu is restored
to human form

so I could strike a sick bird
into a sick man.

In Styhaven, I fed him back to health with pigs' blood,
bacon and pork, the fairy meat of Unland,
while the flower wife and her lover,
sweet on each other, wallowed
in their honeypot.

There was something of the eagle in him still,
the jerky way he'd pick at his clothes,
with a round shine in his eye
that wasn't thinking.

He knew as birds do when it was time
to be somewhere else. One day
we rode to his land,

Blodeuedd tries to
escape

and met her running away,
as if she'd known, too.

If you have seen a blackbird shred a crocus, you'll know
the way he looked at her. They were both my fault,
these crude experiments in human.
I must make something of her
before she was spoiled:

the silence of her movements, for example,
as of many layers of softness
being ruffled by a breeze;
that pale disc of face.

A tap of my wand rearranged her
into the nightgown body
and hooks of an owl.

From now on, she would blossom
only in the dark.

He waited for us where the bathing-house used to be,
the river behind him polishing its stones,
broader and flatter than the pebbles
that a blond boy had spent days
throwing at driftwood.

I noticed the chunky look about his chest,
where he'd put a flat stone down his shirt.
He'd take a blow for a blow,
he said, and stood there,

while the man he'd murdered raised an arm
in an arc like a bird's wing.
The spear passed right through.

You can still see the stone there
with the hole in it.

Gwydion has finished
his story

BY now a consort of snoring of different pitches
is filling the hall. Those who've been listening
have caught the story through a fuddle
of wine and snatches of sleep
as the fire reddened.

Everything seemed to have been torn from its roots,
so that it tumbled over the mind
as in a dream: pigs, seaweed,
birds, people, flowers.

Perhaps that's what he meant by Unland,
a country where things break loose
from their own being.

The storyteller goes on,
as if to himself.

Perhaps he should
tell another?

There's The Man Who Became Someone Else, I could tell that.
It was only for a year, but afterwards
the world had slipped. Things fell through the gaps:
a woman came from nowhere,
a baby vanished . . .

Or The War of the Lonely Queen. A nation
was crushed into ashes for her sake,
but she was lonelier still
when they buried her.

Or The Kidnapped Country, how the fog
lifted the sheep from their fields
and they started again.

As for The Flower-Woman,
that's hocus-pocus.

He resumes the story
of the stolen pigs

He's fighting with the hiccups: The Revenge of the Pigs,
because you don't get fairy meat for nothing –
which reminds me. I was telling you
how I fled to Styhaven
and left the pigs there.

I made my way through the parchment of the woods,
where the sun scattered like candle flames,
yellowing the crackled leaves,
and came to the end,

Y Felenrhyd
(The Yellow Ford)

where a river tripped over itself.
Dismounting on the far side,
I waited for him

till I saw the prickly light
of spears through the trees.

They fight in single
combat; Pryderi has
no chance against
Gwydion's magic

He left his men on the bank, and stepped into the ford:
his strength and a few pounds of steel against one
who could turn his sword to a bramble
or freeze his arm in mid-stroke
with a ringing word.

Pryderi is killed

His blood thinned away, as when you gut a fish.
I thought of how he'd escaped the claw,
survived the shattered cauldron,
the erasing fog.

Prince of the West, who'd lived all his life
on the forested border
of what can't be true,

he lay in the swirling place
where stories begin.